New York City 12/21/16

# MARTHA

a poem

For Stella,

& for glorious dance
& for the grace
the beauty & the
dignity in humanity.

# MARTHA

a poem

Garrett Buhl Robinson

www.garrettrobinson.us

# Table of Contents

## Development           **29**

## Performance                     57

# Emergence

Dance is more than a living art.

Dance is life itself.

## I.i.1

*proem*

We are born of rhythm, an interlinking
sequence of conceptions enmeshed in every
outstretching direction.  Every moment
intends within as we extend throughout.
Each instant is an eternity we
encounter where we discover ourselves
as we will be forever, each moment
expressed to the expanse we understand,
the achievements of agreement in degrees
of correspondence.  Harmonic consonance
arises in the distinct assemblies
strummed in circumstance, plucked with encounters,
warbling together as our vibrant lives
multiply precisely as they coincide,
resonant and reverberant together
in our balanced passages upon the scales.

Martha

**I.i.2**

*conception*

Martha is conceived in tranquility.
From within the innermost recess
of tenderness, stirred by instinctive urge
cultivating upon intricacies
in the diversifying sentience
that elaborates selections upon
recognizing the broadening options
deepening into the foreseeable,
the approach of open offers, the proof
of providence in undeniable
persistence, recognized with assurance
calming and soothing every disturbance
with the undulating luxuries of two
together, and consummated upon
a kiss of consensual acceptance,
in and of this, Martha is conceived.

I.i.3

*the heart's flower*

She grows in rhythm.  The dividing cells,
one from another, elaborately
specialize into the specific parts
that develop the symmetrical whole.
Her mother's blood presses her further open,
a blossom unfolding, outstretching, growing
into the figure of her being, till
Martha's own valved flower blooms, coaxed along
with her Mother's, a tiny echo
in response, an answer within,
distant, almost detached, yet intrinsic,
the fulfillment of life's continuance.
And that tiny flower, the muscular heart,
tirelessly counting the rhythm of life
flowing through the fluency it moves,
touches the tip of each extending appendage.

Martha

## I.i.4

*the mind listening to narratives*

Even before she is aware, she learns.
There is a changing pace of the heart rate,
the labors absorbed through exertions, her
mother ascending the stairs, the jostling,
alternating with each step, climbing, racing.
She hears the windy swell of every breath,
the lungs inflating at her tickling feet
as she floats in a sleepy bubble of growth,
standing on her developing head,
positioned for release to dive into reality,
swaying with each step, until her mother
carefully swings into a seat, sinking
while relaxing, the heart's frantic pace calming,
the pressing heaviness of breath releasing
into the lulling hums of melodies
nimbly stepping through passages of music.

## I.i.5

*first performance*

In this music, she dreams.  This thread leads her,
a mother's comforting voice sweetening in song,
a lullaby buzzing a bubble
imbedded in a warm, floating world.
An unknown opens in conversation.
The sound of another approaching, speaking
away, and then in an affectionate
inflection toward Martha, the changing tone,
a gentle nudging for attention,
the questions punctuated by listening.
Sometimes she responds by stretching a leg
that blunts against her embrace and excites
the surprise of joyous laughter, the signs
of a vitality and attention, the soft
harmonics of involvement a mother
hums from within her deep, sleeping secrets.

Martha

## I.i.6

*limit's end*

What at first had been an immensity,
development has filled beyond comfort.
There is anxiety, and with this, a sense
of the inevitable, a commitment
to bring a new life into the open
through this unstoppable course that the current
arrangement can no longer accommodate.
Martha's heart is ready for her own direction,
her mind buzzes for a world of her own
to continue assembling in the ways
of life outside, the stalwart step of each
infant offspring taking place with the changing
environment through the suppleness
of elastic youth, driving society
into the uncertainty of the future
with the bold growth of new generations.

**I.i.7**

*birth*

There is a struggle with every emergence,
even rising from bed is a daily defiance,
but the first awakening into the world,
plunging through resistance, pressed through a
portal that does not lend itself for easy
passage, is the first great feat of any life;
it is the first great leap to  survive.  Martha
squeezes into an expanding chamber,
her sight, a bright red glow before her unopened
eyes.  Sound, more than a mother's murmurs,
sharpens with the applause in being born,
an ovation in her first breath of air,
filling her lungs, her inner wings that will
flutter inside to loft her life's desires.
She is taken in outstretched hands and curtsies
upon the breast of her mother's calming heart.

## I.ii.1

*distinction of being*

Expelled from her floating chamber to which
she may never return, her first lesson
is resistance. The air moves through her
freely, yet she finds stubborn surfaces
through constant encounters by which
she discovers herself. The immovable masses
become the leverage by which she learns
to move, propelling and pushing her life,
barely lifting her head and outstretching
her examining hands, bringing the world
closer as she brings herself closer
to the world in each focused encounter.
The heart of her mother she had felt
so close, now recedes into a depth
from which she suddenly feels denied
and discovers the heart of her own.

Martha

## I.ii.2

*expression and acceptance*

Martha finds that her every movement
brings joy, her every gesture engages
attention, her most subtle sounds quicken
interest, and even her stinking movements
from within prompt pampering refreshment.
With a whim of breath, her mother offers
herself as warm sustenance and her
father stands over, a strange distance,
stolid reassurance of sheltering
protection.  Every infantile bumble
is an astonishing accomplishment,
every inarticulate utterance
a grandiloquent declaration
enrapturing an audience suspended
to support her development and is
overjoyed with her simple existence.

## I.ii.3

*expression and connection*

The voices that had grown familiar
and she had heard through the liquid distance
suddenly appear.  Where before she had heard
of the world from within another,
now she encounters immediately.
She witnesses those invisible sounds
now arising from their origins, tones
attached to gesturing expressions,
the questions inquiring with promptings
of the simplest emotions that move the earth
around her with responding assurance,
where any reaction is an astounding
understanding.  Then, as she witnesses
the intricacies of interaction,
she easily learns the references
as she is the center of attention.

Martha

## I.ii.4

*creating understanding*

Turning her attention from others, those
whose greatest joy seems to be watching her
smile, she begins filling her world with her
senses, broadening herself through each encounter.
She earnestly pries open her eyes into
the blinding bright daylight that softens in
acceptance of discernment distinguishing
her surroundings in everything she may reach,
clasping to conform reality in
a grasp of tender fingers molding into
the shapes raised to her examining eyes
so her mind connects itself with the world
in recreations of recognition.
Through this, the world gives, offering itself
in investigative impressions,
openly unfolding in her interest.

## I.ii.5

*distinguishing the world*

Martha learns early the ways of navigating
through life, bouncing and bounding through others'
reactions, the different ways of being
recognized and received, the capacity
of one's grasp and the firmness of attachment.
She speaks, as she hears others, through summons
for attention expressing intent
and significance.  As she distinguishes
components and their relevance, she
builds within herself her rendition
of existence composed of her awareness.
Then, through this, she shares herself through her
attention, devoted through her instilled
interest, curious and luminous.
She grows and develops by reassembling
the world inside herself through understanding.

Martha

**I.ii.6**

*meshing perspectives*

She builds her speech upon identities.
The information is the material
for the process, the push and pull of her
development.  The material,
real and imaginary, is linked by the arching
leap between what is and what she comprehends.
She shares her sequence of speech, her world,
not as she perceives, but as she may
articulate and communicate.
Those places of related reference she
had been shown, she now shows, opening her own
world for others, explaining the arrangements,
her own assortment of the familiar components
in the disposition of her character.
Through this, along a path of references,
she attempts to sustain other's attention.

**I.ii.7**

*learning to walk*

She has stood, her hands clasped by her parents.
They have lifted her arms to pull her legs
and her feet beneath her, and slowly shifted
her weight upon them, the wobbly stilts
strengthening beneath her, to carry her
with this awkward novelty, to learn to move
with her own will and follow her own vision.
Eventually she stands on her own, her tiny
legs lifting her before she plops back to the ground.
Standing again, she sees her mother's arms
outstretched, beckoning to receive her.
Rather quickly, she is able to overcome
the encumbered steps of her new existence
and plots along the measured distance,
extending her first musical rendition
in a melodious accomplishment.

**I.iii.1**

*from pleads to declarations*

Martha speaks in rhythms, pleas to be fed
or cleaned, pleas of increasing specificity
through vocabularies applied to other's
attention and interest as she explores
the ways of correspondence.  With her new
mobility, she broadens her inquiries
expressed in silence through contemplation,
the calm receptiveness of inquiry,
revolving thoughts as objects to be viewed
from various perspectives, the insights
that peek around obstructions as her image
of the world alters through her movement.
The objects change in shape and arrangement
as she moves beyond the mere identities
and recognizes their associations
as she turns her pleads into declarations.

Martha

## I.iii.2

*the vacancies between understanding*

Venturing further, Martha begins
to experience a world that becomes
increasingly reluctant and resistant.
From her experiences of effortless
acceptance where her every gesture was
celebrated in hearty amusement,
she finds that not all the world is open
for easy welcome.  Her fingers, still
developing agility and strength,
fumble some objects that drop and fall,
and that which she admires sometimes shatters
in irretrievable loss.   And not everyone
she meets is pleased with her childish babbling
and she is perplexed at their baffled expressions,
finding there is more distance than simple space
to overcome and reach others in understanding.

## I.iii.3

*impressions of sound*

Sounds signal movement with the impetus
of pressure, of approach, of impending
presence undulating in waves of vibrations,
thrumming the air with agitated
excitement. With the ear's sensitivity
Martha attunes herself with her environment,
coordinating her life with the signals
of activity, the announcements
of displacement and engagement.
Her parents talk, the cars pass, the birds sing,
the world speaks its being, emanating
through the air expanding with recognition,
pooling in the resonance of memory
settling within impressions, and reflecting
a way, her way, through her own life and mind,
in which she learns to move through this arrangement.

Martha

## I.iii.4

*movement speaks*

She broadens with each contact, the lives
of others she encounters, turning her
world through the interactions, creating
dispositions, orientations, and ways
to navigate without disruption,
evoking excitement, stimulating
the joy of her receptions, fulfilling
expectations especially those for surprise,
to present the renewal of the unknown,
to show the novelty of the unforeseen,
to open the wonders of discovery
found in every instance and which Martha
brings forth without reluctance
in effortless abundance, a confluence
of refreshment with every step rippling
with mercurial messages.

## I.iii.5

*tones of movement*

She teaches herself different ways to speak
in her movement, whispering delicate
steps to approach without disturbance.
The birds accept her careful curiosity
so that she nearly touches the flash of wings
and feels the rush of air in their lift
that carry her pursuing sight through their flight.
With the familiar – family and friends – she learns
the directness, the shortest distance, with
convivial vibrance that is greeted
with the greatest reception.  Or on occasions
when her mother is busy, her somber
steps through the house's corridors allure
subtle interest with their solemn wanders.
She learns the ways to engage and carry
other's attention upon her movements.

Martha

## I.iii.6

*life lives*

When she speaks, she displaces the world around
her in discourses with others.  She explains
what she sees, what she feels, what she
discovers, and extends each open end
of her curiosity in an inquiry
of the variety of ways the world
makes sense as it is shared
through the related ways of correspondence.
Yet before and beyond representations,
she finds truer expression in movement.
When she moves, there is the immediacy
of reality, not as it is said,
but as it is.  With her steps, distance
diminishes and the world approaches in earnest.
Charging, retreating, embracing, she moves
in what is exactly as she feels it.

**I.iii.7**

*first lift*

Sometimes her father lifts her and spins her
giggling with elation through  the air.
The moment of flight, extending upon
the distinct, a leap suspended in disbelief,
the rush of air like the wind beneath wings,
lofted upon another's attention,
fixed upon her father's open eyes
and happy smile, the joy released to please
exhilarating and free, watching the world
whirl, turning into an exciting blur
moving in union, together,
blending into a thick mist of excited
delight, a tranquil stillness through the rush
of soaring heights.  Then, eventually set
to return upon the firm surface of the earth,
her outstretching arms persuade, "Again, again."

# Development

We never become what we wish.

We become what we practice.

**II.i.1**

*to stand*

Martha's first lesson in dance is how to stand.
Only in the most tranquil stillness can
one completely capture movement that passes
through forms fixed in the immediate, framed
in the instant of each position's presence.
The patience in waiting is an active
realization as Martha reflects upon
the height of her life, not simply her thoughts
and her feet, but her whole body in harmony.
Before she can move, she must levitate
from where she stands, floating and opening
with the spanning grandeur of a tree
from where she may learn to move with the ease
of the breeze, each step extending free,
based upon the reliance of the other's strength,
more than boundless, but in natural balance.

Martha

## II.i.2

*to stand continued*

In standing properly there is dignity,
an elegant alignment where the body
is its own compliment and carriage,
that even when the heart thrums with a team
of horses and the brain buzzes like a honeyed
hive of bees, the body entire and complete
is aplomb with assured ease.   Martha
stands on a mountain of accomplishments
accumulated through her dedicated
concentration and from the sharpened tip
of the lofty peak, she can see everything.
Her stillness is filled with excitement
as if the body is ecstatically composed
of a million wings fluttering in a flurry
of anticipated flight, devotion
opening every possibility.

**II.i.3**

*to stretch*

Her lessons reintroduce her to herself
each day, her elastic youth bending in
ways she had never considered, shaping
and developing her life through  an art.
Each day she presses herself to her limits
and intensely strains to overcome them,
and broadens her life through discovering
the unexpected.  Conscious of her breath,
thoughtful of the placement of every step,
the passage becomes the destination,
sustaining movement — the accomplishment,
deliberation — the objective through
the embrace of space available and filled
as she stretches her life through changing shapes
that transform like the expressive letters
scripted across the bright page of each day.

Martha

## II.i.4

*to connect*

Taking shape as an elegant vase
of composure, Martha fills herself
with the fluid of a dancer, connecting
the positions with transitions, assembling
the phrases into fluent statements.
When she opens her arms, she embraces
the world; with the nod of her head,
the room darkens with ominous weight;
then lifting her eyes wide, spring arrives,
her closed arms become a trembling bud
on the verge of bursting to bloom,
and as it does, it floods with luscious layers
of delicate petals pouring forth exhaustless,
making the ways of refreshing rivers
she releases in the rush of her movement,
an unstoppable existence.

## II.i.5

*to turn*

Through her movement she turns, whirling,
spinning upon the tips of her toes
to reel the world in while flinging it forth,
balanced, confronting every direction
at once, revolving deeper into
the immediate through a course that pulses
to refresh and replenish every part,
relentlessly spinning in controlled abandon
then slowing, ponderous, delicate, a celestial
immensity of a spiraling galaxy.
She is at peace within the motion,
the ferocious hurricane's tranquil eye
holding the faithful boldness of David,
fearless, beneath the whirling sling
before the giant, the spin of a fixed image
as she draws in all her surroundings.

Martha

## II.i.6

*to leap*

Her sense of the floor becomes natural,
her life a continuity of feeling
from the heights of her mind to the tips
of her toes.   She is aware of the earth
from which she rose and continues to rise
in fanciful flights of loft lifted, seemingly
effortless, upon the concealed labors
of years, all her personal struggles
endured and embraced with the resilience
of her being, so that through her performance,
she reveals only what delights and astonishes.
She has privately endeared herself
to the humility of the ground, to the base
weight of reality, offered the bounty of her
time and attention, so that she does not walk,
she floats, she does not run, she flows

## II.i.7

*the leap*

and upon her momentous strides,
covering the ground with her attention,
each step an upright assurance,
the print of her feet, the counting sounds
of measured steps leveling any difference,
drawing in distance with the gliding stride
of a conquering cadence, so the raising
of her foot lifts the floor to beg for her
return, the curved breadth of the earth opens
to receive, the horizons retreat so
the sky may more fully witness to see,
the world beckoning her in acceptance,
rising beneath her to lift her
with a suspending intensity
upon the taut bow of exertion
for the arrow's release in a breathtaking leap.

**II.ii.1**

*the distant world*

Even through her youth, Martha has grown
accustomed to travel.  In a life of motion,
she even moves in her sleep, napping
in exhaustion in cars, vans, buses
and the numbing  hum of soaring planes.
At times, life feels to be a revolving
carnival where nothing can be held
for more than a moment, where everything
slips away as she is pulled in every direction
for performances and auditions, the flashing
flourish of festivals that quickly disassemble
to a scuttling clutter as everyone leaves.
Friendships are often brief as gathered classes
pass, and others are only heard from
in distant rumors no one can ever
believe with myths of boyfriends and prom queens.

Martha

## II.ii.2

*morning lake*

Martha fondly remembers early mornings
on her way to class before school.
They left in the cold darkness before day
and their route took them past a lake, sometimes
just as dawn would break.  The gossamer drift
of mist appeared as if the water was
mingling in the sky, rising in cumulous
billows imbued with the hues that first warmed
the eyes before the blazing globe bloomed and rose.
There were swans sometimes, wild swans.
Her mother told her some swans were kept
by clipping their wings, but these swans
returned because they wanted to.  When they break,
snow returning to the sky,  the ripples
broaden like the rings of an audience upon a surface
so smooth, she knew she could dance across it.

## II.ii.3

*rehearsal hells*

Passing through youth in the rehearsal hall's
space between barres, she sometimes thought
of the corridors of others that must be
rows of windows that open wide outside
in the relaxed laughter of carefree release.
Yet, her corridors were walled with mirrors,
the repeating reflections extending
into a critiquing infinity
obsessively scrutinizing details
till she appears at ease even when every
fiber of her life is straining to scream
and the spanning arch of her foot is shaped
to outstretch nothing less than the impossible.
Yet how can she turn her back on this, when dance
has become her whole existence, her life
entire dedicated to an art, only
and rarely appreciated on the stage.

Martha

## II.ii.4

*slippers*

Everyone passes, even teachers, as motion
through music, each sound drawing her
further, the measured count of each step,
phrasing the passages through persistence
along a path to an uncertain distance.
Her foundation, her affectionate parents,
disappear into an enlarging audience
though she seeks at each révérence before
the impassable rift of the curtain's close.
She has begun to grow closest to her
slippers.  They move too and they are always
with her, every day, everywhere.  They wear,
they are replaced, but somehow always the same,
the snug, accustomed fit, the sheen of silk,
the rituals of these ribbon laced gifts,
the petals of the flowers she dances through.

**II.ii.5**

*the art of civilization*

One day, after school and returning to class,
she is surprised to find a trip is planned,
a short drive into the city.   Riding in the van,
she is familiar with the roads.  Moving
through the velocity, she listens to music,
seeing the fingers' lyrical steps upon
the cello's frets and even in her seat she dances,
her feet moving, her hands gesturing directions
as her mind whirls through the music.
Her life is motion upon motions, movement
upon movements, each step venturing further
from the surge of every momentous
accomplishment, extending continuous
through history and leading into the future
made and sustained into our reality
through the linking lives of performers.

Martha

## II.ii.6

*another glimpse at the distant world*

They pass a park and she sees children
her age playing, running across a field
without a thought of the placement of each
step, only concerned with finding the closest
sources of enjoyment.  There is a pool.
The surface of the water is ruffled with play
as the children splash and laugh
as their lives weave and entwine without
the simplest concern for posture, slouched
and slumped as they relax, endearingly
leaning upon one another, hanging out
without need for composure.  A couple sits
at a park bench with no other concern
but their embrace together, with nothing
else to do but feel each other's touch.
For Martha, all this solemnly passes.

**I.ii.7**

*the theater's facade*

Arriving at the greatest theater in the city,
Ms. Kennedy leads Martha and the others
to the front entrance and says, "This is
an awesome sight I am sure you have all
seen before.  It is built to be seen
from a distance, designed to allure
and entice, not for idleness, but for fulfillment.
It is designed to tower and impress,
but not to intimidate, but instead
to open with outstretching welcome.
This entrance is majestic, offering
accommodations that will entertain
and enrich with the wonders of life
that the audience will find performed inside.
But from now on my dears, you all will enter
this building from a different direction."

**II.iii.1**

*artist's entrance*

From the theater's entrancing grandeur
they walk around the side of the building
to an exposed and ruddy brick wall at the back.
Ms. Kennedy approaches the shadowy
descent of stairs that appear to be
cut from a slab of concrete, and swinging
the door open with the hinges complaining,
she stoops through the threshold to step inside.
She waves her arm to signal the others to come.
Inside, Martha sees a long hallway, far
from glamorous, extending into the subterranean
recesses inside.  The walls are lined with
exposed conduits and pipes and the bulbs
of light are set in cages for protection
when heavy equipment is moved.  The space
speaks of the bare necessity of utility.

Martha

## II.iii.2

*hallway, principal's dressing room*

Ms. Kennedy explains. "Don't expect
any glamour here. That is reserved
for the stage. Even the Green Room is
more of a coat check than a posh salon."
She guides her students through the labyrinth,
although it appears more like a catacombs,
and says, "Don't worry about the eerie
quiet now. During the production this
place is hopping and teaming with life, but it is
the bustle of work. This is not the place
of showcase." She then turns to open
a door and they all squeeze inside, barely
fitting in the tiny chamber with little
more than a diva mirror and a bunk.
"And this is the dressing room for the principal.
See, the luxury of a private shower."

## II.iii.3

*the principal's seat*

Ms. Kennedy has each of them sit in turn
and gaze into the mirror as she explains,
"I want you all to see yourselves sitting here.
In the mirror you may see the reflection
of all the dancers before you, radiant
masters of their art, thrilled before the performance.
But the dancer's place is not a seat,
the dancer's place is the dance, and you will rise
from this cloud of fluttering butterflies
and find your place upon the stage, and once
the music begins to play, you will
feel the sweeping sense of freedom in movement.
In electrified excitement, before
your own brilliant debuts, all of you may sit
at this seat in pristine preparation,
and one day, some of you most certainly will."

Martha

## II.iii.4

*general dressing room*

Then she leads them into the general
dressing room.  "And here is where you will
begin.  This is the place of the corps
of the company, the body of the being
that moves in ranging intricacy
from supportive studies and tireless training
into the essence and entirety
of a singularly expressive entity
that speaks through movement in a language
that is not only of life, but is life.
In these rudimentary chambers
that are lined with the conduits  and pipes
like the veins and arteries of the building,
there is no doubt that you all are the heart
and soul of this theater and this living art.
Now put on your slippers and follow me."

**II.iii.5**

*deeper into the passages*

Having stepped in their slippers, the dancers
follow their instructor through the passages
that blindly wind through the unknown.  Without
certainty of where the passage leads,
everything is dimly foreign and cold.
The walls become caverns staging wavering
shadows that extend from Martha
and blend with everyone else as they
walk through austere haunts of empty echoes.
They follow Ms. Kennedy who leads
with her assured and purposeful head held high.
She turns to climb a set of steps and commands
them to take care as they ascend and then
arranges them in a line in the dark.
Unable to see, yet without the need,
Martha can sense an awesome openness.

Martha

## II.iii.6

*the edge of the stage*

Suddenly the lights blare and the curtained
stage glows before them.  Ms. Kennedy
says, "I know all of you have found me tough
through the years, critiquing relentlessly,
while applauding sparingly.  You all deserve
applause, and you all will receive it, you
all have earned it, but remember, in applause
you may find approval and assurance,
but you will not find strength and through the past
few years, strength is what you all needed most.
After you graduate from this school, your
challenges in your careers and your lives
are only beginning.  Never forget
that the most difficult test is success.
This stage you now see is not empty; this
stage is filled with every possibility."

**II.iii.7**

*upon the stage*

Ms. Kennedy waves the dancers onto
the stage as she steps to the side and out
of their way.  Some immediately burst
into the open, others make delicate
steps as if feeling their way on a hairbreadth
path only they may see themselves.
To Martha, the stage feels as familiar
as rehearsal with the draping curtain
closing the corridor.  Ms. Kennedy says,
"Ladies" while pointing down the stage
as the curtain suddenly lifts.  The whole
universe opens before their eyes
that climb in flight and rise above the balconies
in the engulfing rush of open space.
At center stage, her eyes firmly fixed
on the future, Martha pirouettes.

# Performance

Dancers are the poets in the language of life.

## III.i.1

*existence and movement*

Movement is the essence of existence,
the first expression and endless answer.
We exist and we move, and for the length
of our life, and beyond our lives, we move.
Our life, to its greatest development,
is determined in how we move together.
As individual and organism
in a unity of dynamic complements,
coupling and combining to create,
gathering and grouping to perpetuate,
organized upon interest, converging
and overlapping where we aggregate,
multi-eyed, multi-limbed,  striding through time
in successive generations, processing
in endurance and agreement, we move
in interactions with our environment.

Martha

## III.i.2

*origins of dance*

Our myths and our beliefs were assembled
through movement, dancing around bonfires
like planets around the sun,  pulsing through
the radiance while extending into
the unknown, alluring, accumulating
while broadening our satellite circles.
Enjoying and participating, we
embody our beliefs, parts of a whole
creating our cohesive societies,
moving through our desires in the music
we make, sustaining our interactions
in articulation and understanding,
our comprehension  in our agreement,
the rapture and ecstasy shaping
a revolving unity, balanced upon
what we are and all that we may be.

### III.i.3

*mythic imagination in movement*

In those night's aglow with ingenuity,
moving with the cadence of music,
we reenacted our imagination
through the forms of our being and involvement.
The light would stream in the surrounding trees
as if dancing themselves with Orpheus singing.
We would stalk mythic creatures that would sustain
and renew us.  We drank from fountains flowing
from mystic mountains that arduously climbed
into the heavens.  We found the bounty
of fruit, the succulent nourishment
of arboreal offerings we gathered
through ourselves and our activity.
We wove and knitted our lives, braided
like twining lines, extending and strengthening
together in ways we could cinch and climb.

Martha

## III.i.4

*company and union*

Through the humbling struggles of majestic
movement, Martha is accepted
by a company.  Deep beneath the glamour,
embroiled with the work, she nimbly
steps into her burgeoning involvement.
Beneath the burden of the exceptional,
as she is asked, she performs and slips easily
from the awkwardness of the unfamiliar
into her element and essence of dance,
the language they all understand and speak
and sing in the music of their movement,
whistling in the wind in the air they stir
through the straight and the sinuous paths they
create with their steps through passages they carve
through space in forms that excite and invite
in the dance of the world that moves through them.

**III.i.5**

*understudy*

Through the dance and lengthy rehearsals
she learns of others, stretching together,
the shared postures of their individual lives,
the unity of the practice, the ensembles
with one another, the experience they share
in the camaraderie they build.  As an
understudy, she follows the steps of others,
gesturing with their motions, a shadow
of those lofty figures of experience who
have already found their way deep
into this art through practice and performance
and have risen on stages through countless
productions in  town and on tour while always
at home in the dance.  In this Martha
learns, exploring herself under others
until she may arise in and of her own.

Martha

## III.i.6

*member of the corps*

Each day, each performance is a stretch
further, a step higher, another increment
as she broadens herself, extending her life
through experience and understanding,
stepping through barriers of the unknown,
gliding on bright smiles even through aches
and devastating heartbreaks; breathing calmly,
even if verging to collapse from exhaustion;
maintaining the graceful lines arching
through the performances for the audience's
enjoyment, and even in the back,
practically a piece of the scenery while
the principals perform, she shoulders
the weight of expectations with the others,
and carries the audience with the ease
of each evening into the dawns of their delight.

**III.i.7**

*a dance, the dance*

Dancing with others within the light's heat,
through the fluent flow of the music,
within the setting  of every scene,
Martha danced within herself, within her dreams,
within the company and within the audience
extending in every direction of her
involvement.  She danced the dance of her life,
the passion of her intense mind aspiring
with her desire with the  whole company
supporting one another, broadening
into the audience, touching the whole
city by inspiring the community
while spinning on rising pinnacles,
changing the shape of space between them,
drawing all into a dance that is now
in a movement together forever.

**III.ii.1**

*rivalry with obscurity*

In the company, the friendship is fierce,
the competition is relentless,
but their competition is not as much
against each other, but against oblivion
where even the slightest stumble may be
overwhelmed by the caustic dissolution
of obscurity.  They have all dedicated
their entire lives to developing themselves,
sacrificed their childhood in discipline
toward an excellence and perfection
of movement.  They are all poised to leap
at any moment through the narrowest
opening to seize opportunity,
not through sabotage but by surpassing
expectations and reaching prominence
by accomplishing the impossible.

Martha

## III.ii.2

*moving statues*

The champions dance as if on fire,
radiating a vibrant brilliance
that commands everyone's attention
so no one can take their eyes from their place
on the stage.  Every gesture resonates
profoundly, their form a fluency
of moving statues where every instance
is a timeless position of physical
perfection to show how life feels
living in the greatest intensity.
When they leap, the audience soars; when they
reach with longing arms, the audience receives
their embrace; when they spin, the audience's
attention is sharpened to a precise
focus where everyone's interest converges
in the most appealing agreement.

## III.ii.3

*beauty and utility*

The programs are always composed
with careful consideration, reading
the community's expectations and tastes,
drawing the audience with what's accustomed
while performing the invaluable service
of challenging conventions and exposing,
even in discomfort, the openness
of the unknown where we may continue to grow.
Then combining the staples of the seasons,
sustaining tradition and identity
while not ignoring new possibilities,
balancing the expected delicacies
with courageous uncertainties
to broaden and transform in development
between the stability of the familiar
and the refreshment of premiers.

Martha

## III.ii.4

*relentless commitment*

Through these alterations, outside funding
favors that can restrain a person
from performing with the arbitrary
maneuvering that is less about dance
than frivolous politics, Martha overcomes
all this with persistence, where even mountains
of resistance succumb with attrition
against her relentless movement.  She had
long decided that through every practice,
and even in the humblest parts of productions,
she would dance as if her life depended on it.
Even in voluntary service amongst
school children, she demonstrates dance
as if for her company's board of trustees,
knowing, they will, but yet young, be the future
audience for the art that is her life.

## III.ii.5

*lonely star*

Through the years, she ascends the ranks,
answering every challenge with her
accomplishments, learning that through
her increased prominence she becomes
more exposed and vulnerable, so that
the demands intensify with pressure
upon every aspect of her life.  Attention
and its treacheries do not differentiate
between the professional and the personal,
and even concentrates upon the private
to degrees of trespassing, seeking the tender
humanity behind her stellar performances.
She persists and follows the lessons of her
art, and applies it to her life, deciding
that when she leaps, she leaps boldly,
and when she lands, she lands gently.

Martha

## III.ii.6

*the dance of life*

Knowing that her art has brought her to her
success, she concentrates more upon it.  Even
her personal involvements are carefully
choreographed disciplines of discretion
with attention minding every subtlety.
She finds there is a robust delicacy
in life, a balance of careful deliberation,
the magnificent movement achieved
in the guidance of practice, and upon
the intensely familiar she finds the firm basis
from which she may extend into the novel,
knowing her achievements in dance open
doors, yet careful not to let them close
behind her and cut her away from her source.
And when people protest, "All you do is dance."
Martha answers, "Because I am a dancer."

## III.ii.7

*Martha's dance is everyone's dance*

Eventually, Martha achieves one
of the highest honors – a dance commissioned
for her.  A dance that complements
and celebrates her style.  Through the years
she has made many characters her own,
and those characters have become part of her
in the continued assembly of her
elaborately unique unity
of enriched expression that can adjust
to any challenge, that has persevered
before every resistance and surpassed
every obtuse obstacle.  And more
than the inspiration, more than the model,
she is the source of the creation,
collaborator of the composition
along with everyone in attendance.

## III.iii.1

*opening night*

On the night of the world premiere the crowd
is a storm outside thundering with grumbles
of flashing speculations, stirring with nervous
energy at the opaque face of the strange
and unexpected.  Without knowing how
they will feel through the ensuing debut,
they dangle from a cliff, waving their legs
trying to touch their toes somewhere they may
stand while trading predictions they relate
from their previous experiences.
Then, they fan to their seats with their programs
enclosing rehearsal photos and the title:
*I Stand on a Rock in the Noon Day Sun.*
The lobby chimes sound, the entrance lights blink,
the doors carefully and silently close,
sealing the whispers inside the theater.

Martha

## III.iii.2

*the dance begins*

Upon the stage, Martha stands in her place
and waits.  Her body is lunging to move
in every direction at once.  Beyond the curtain,
the clatter of clapping then a sudden hush.
The conductor stands upon the podium,
a glowing figure in the darkness before
the sparkling polish of the instruments.
At one moment, there is perfect silence,
as if space was the surface of a placid lake.
The speaker announces, "In humanity
I see grace, beauty and dignity.
Here.  Let me show you."  Then the curtain
lifts with the rush of Niagara.  The music
moves, filling the openness with consoling
tones, a melody of the woods twirling
ribbons of wind and gently, the dance begins.

**III.iii.3**

*Martha's dance*

With calm assurance Martha offers her
first step, committed to the performance.
The anxious jitters she had felt are gone.
They were not a sense of reluctance;
they were the irritation of restraint.
Through her practice, dance is more than natural,
it is hardly an effort, it is more
than even her life, it is liberation.
She communicates with the crowd, she feels
their attention and responds with movement,
drawing them to her with the promise of lift
as if she could carry the whole city,
and on nights like this she does as they rise
into heights of harmonious beauty.
Her steps embolden others and her reach
touches their hearts that suddenly rush with love.

Martha

## III.iii.4

*Martha's partner*

Martha's partner arrives, bounding on the stage
and nimbly leaping in circles around her
with such magnificence, even she must pause.
Standing, he is a solid mountain she may climb,
a strength that is firm, but does not hurt, stern
and reliant, so she can jump into his lifts
to soar open and free, as if he sets her
in the sky where she floats effortlessly.
They dance together as a singular body,
converging and fusing through the music,
assembling with the audience till the entire
setting is a single, living sensation.
Then, extending from her partner's clasp, they turn
with their eyes fixed upon one another,
their deepening gaze speaking volumes,
and what they say, the audience understands.

**III.iii.5**

*Martha's dance continues*

Her dance is ferocious, devouring space
and filling the void with a flood of life.
The fullness of her movement is overwhelming,
pressing the audience back in their seats
as they witness in disbelief as she
achieves the impossible with ease.
She is a wave on a torrential river,
a form fixed upon a relentless movement,
a surge that splashes over any distance
and sends rippling shivers up the rows of seats
in water lines that engulf the balconies
and even mountains drown as she climbs
through clouds above oceans overflowing.
Her eyes glowing with otherworldly ecstasy,
she moves in a wild, refined release
that is the truest achievement of liberty.

Martha

## III.iii.6

*Martha's dance continues*

Every moment she presses further as she
stretches through limits, bursting through barriers,
filling every  instant with all that is possible.
As she extends, each step is a new life,
a blossom from which she springs
budding and bursting from unpeeling petals,
shedding and disrobing layers that cover
and restrain her being from achieving
the truest expression of her essence –
to move without resistance, frictionless flight,
molting her shadows with her radiance,
chasing the shades away with blazing vitality
igniting brilliant light in every one's eyes
till all the audience stands on their toes
as if her indomitable life might
leap free from her exhausted body.

## III.iii.7

*révérence*

The audience roars and jumps to their feet
with unhesitant approval, convinced
of having witnessed unsurpassable
excellence.  Not only did they see what
they can still hardly believe, that Martha
not only flew, but she carried them with her,
to reveal a vision of achievement,
not only of the human spirit
without limit, but the overflowing
fulfillment through involvement and enjoyment.
She offered all, and withheld nothing, and now
she is carried upon the ovation.
After the curtain drops Martha must be
helped to walk away, having expended
everything without even reserving
enough energy to leave the stage.

## About the Poet

Garrett Buhl Robinson was born and raised in Trussville, Alabama.  At sixteen he was introduced to formal poetry and has been obsessed with lyrical verse ever since.

At a young age, he was introduced to dance through poetry.  He remains a passionate and dedicated supporter of the art.

He lives in New York City.

www.garrettrobinson.us

## Other books by Garrett Buhl Robinson

A Novel by
**Garrett Buhl Robinson**

In the middle of the night, a young man walks to the railroad tracks. From a nearby switchyard, he catches hold of a coal train that carries him from his home and from himself. In time, he comes to realize that he is not on his own, but that he is a small, yet essential portion of a vast and wondrous continuum. Travelling through the country, he composes letters for his childhood friend.

These are his letters for life.
These are his letters of love.
These are his letters to Zoë.

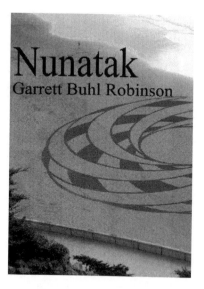

Nunatak
Garrett Buhl Robinson

Do nice guys finish last?

Evan Moore struggles through the breathtaking wilderness of Alaska and a summer job working in a salmon cannery to find out that life is not a game.

Through his interactions with others, he learns that life is a musical language that flourishes as it is sustained. There is no race. There is no finish. The real challenge is to survive, not alone, but in the refreshing novelties of our differences.

This nice guy is built to last.

Made in the USA
Middletown, DE
09 June 2016